Adult coloring book

stress relieving designs for relaxation

This book
belongs to

_____

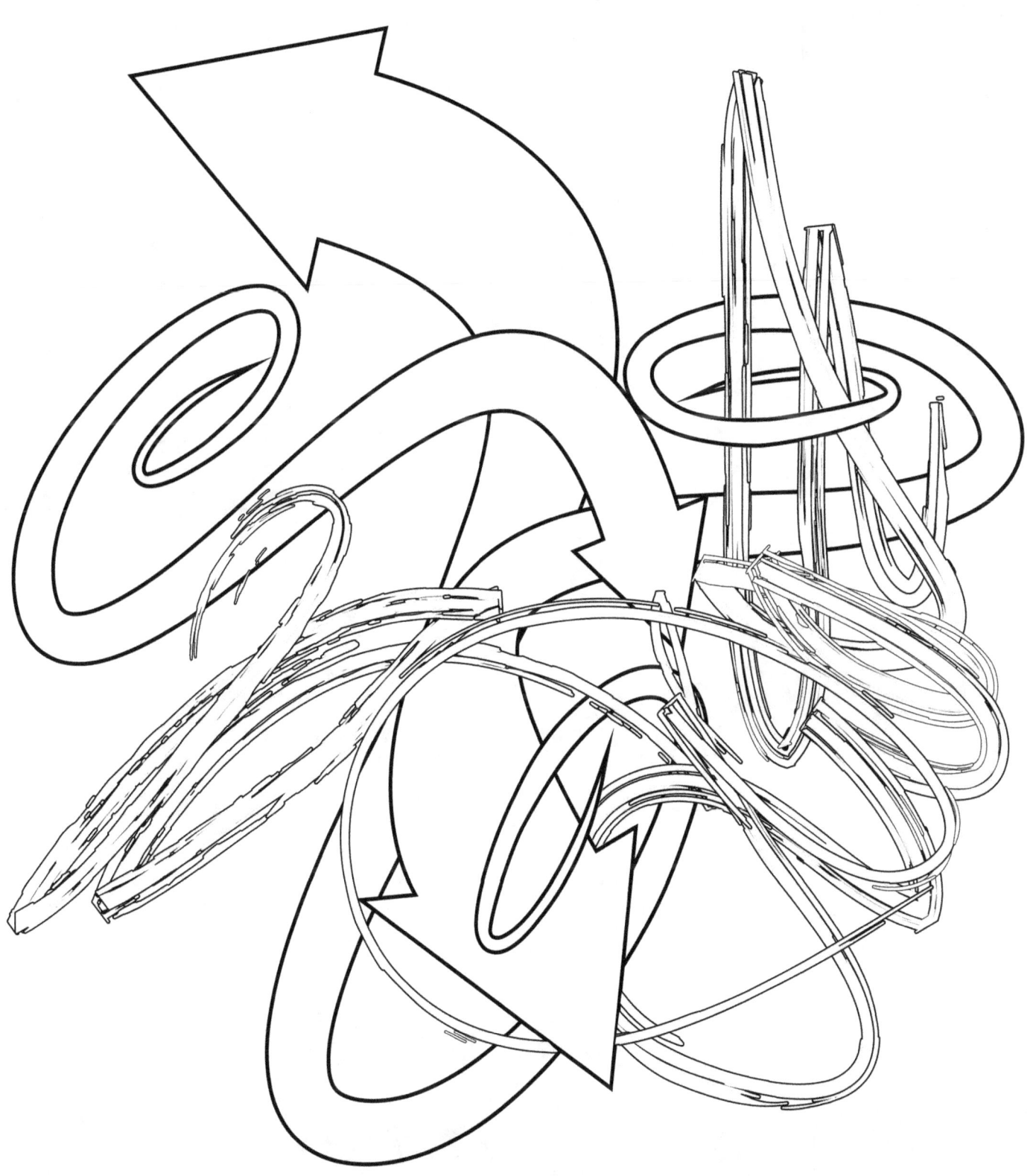

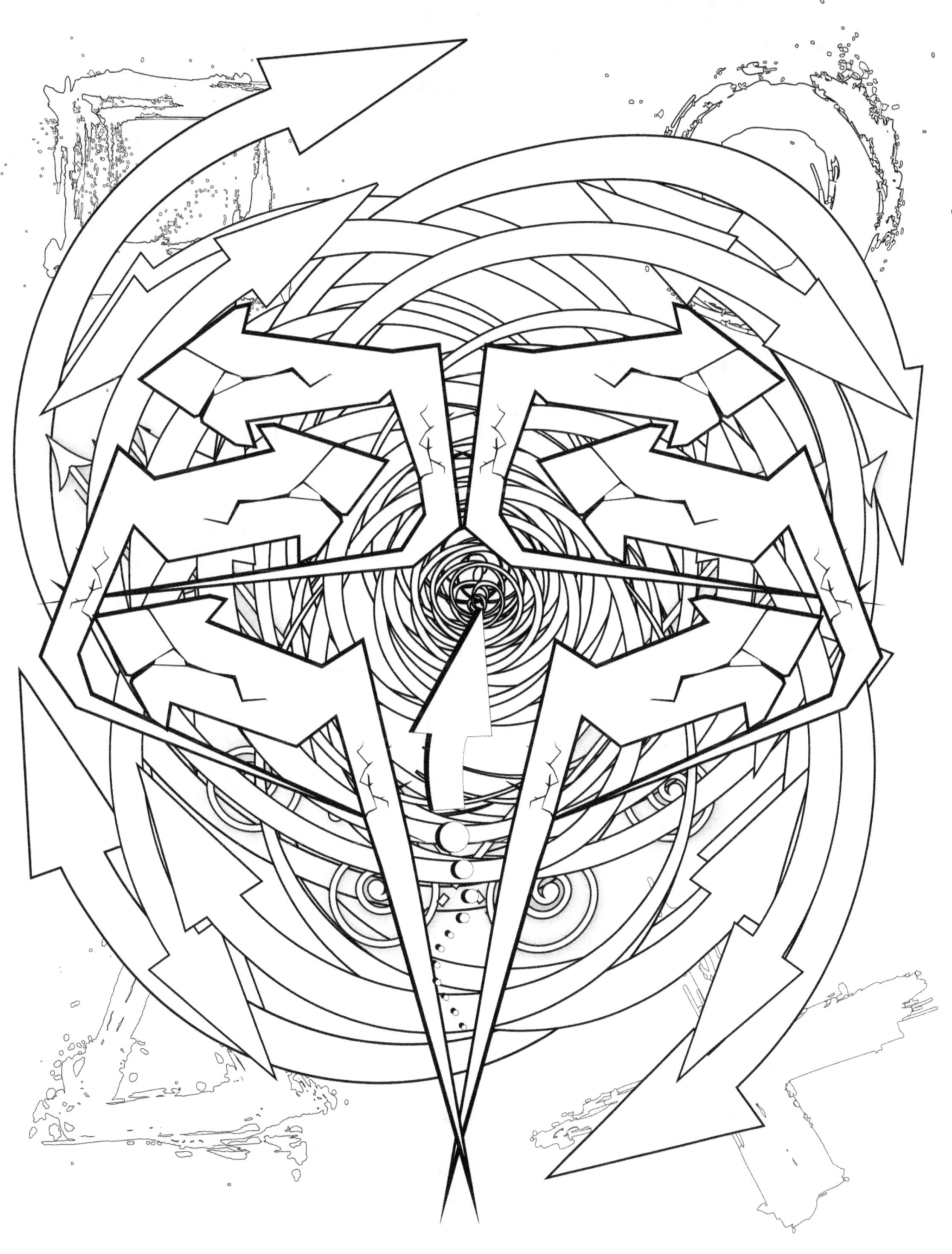

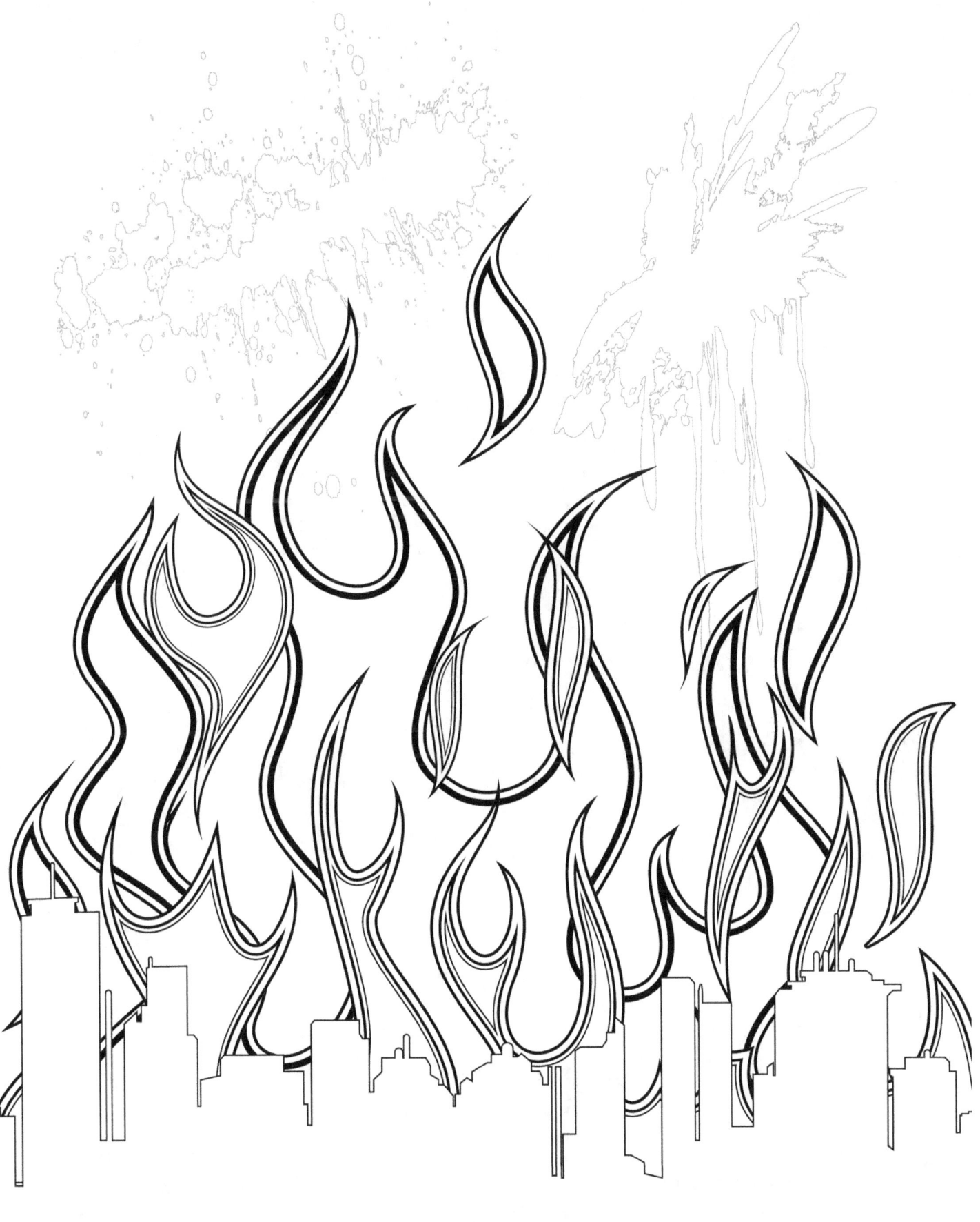

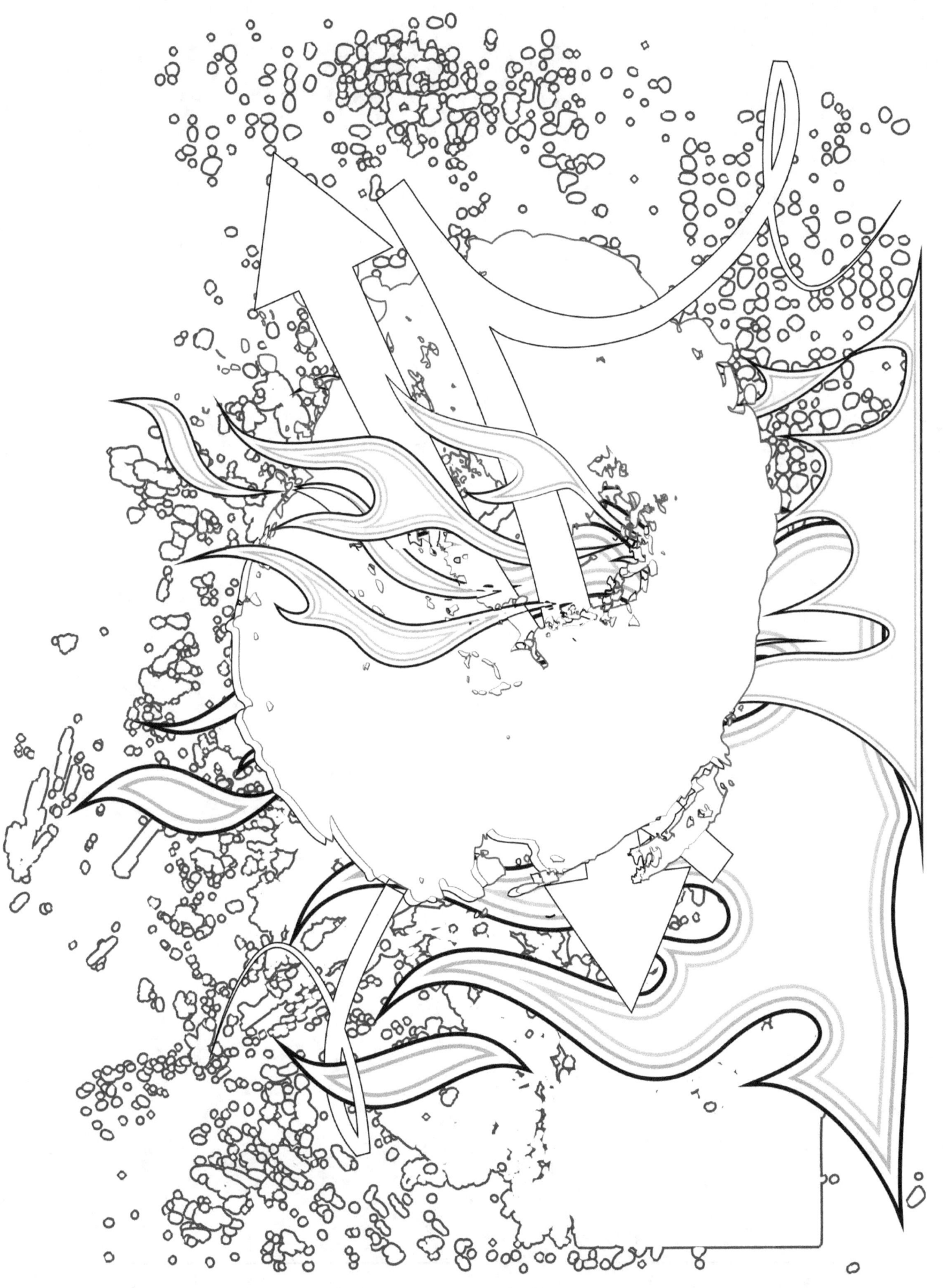

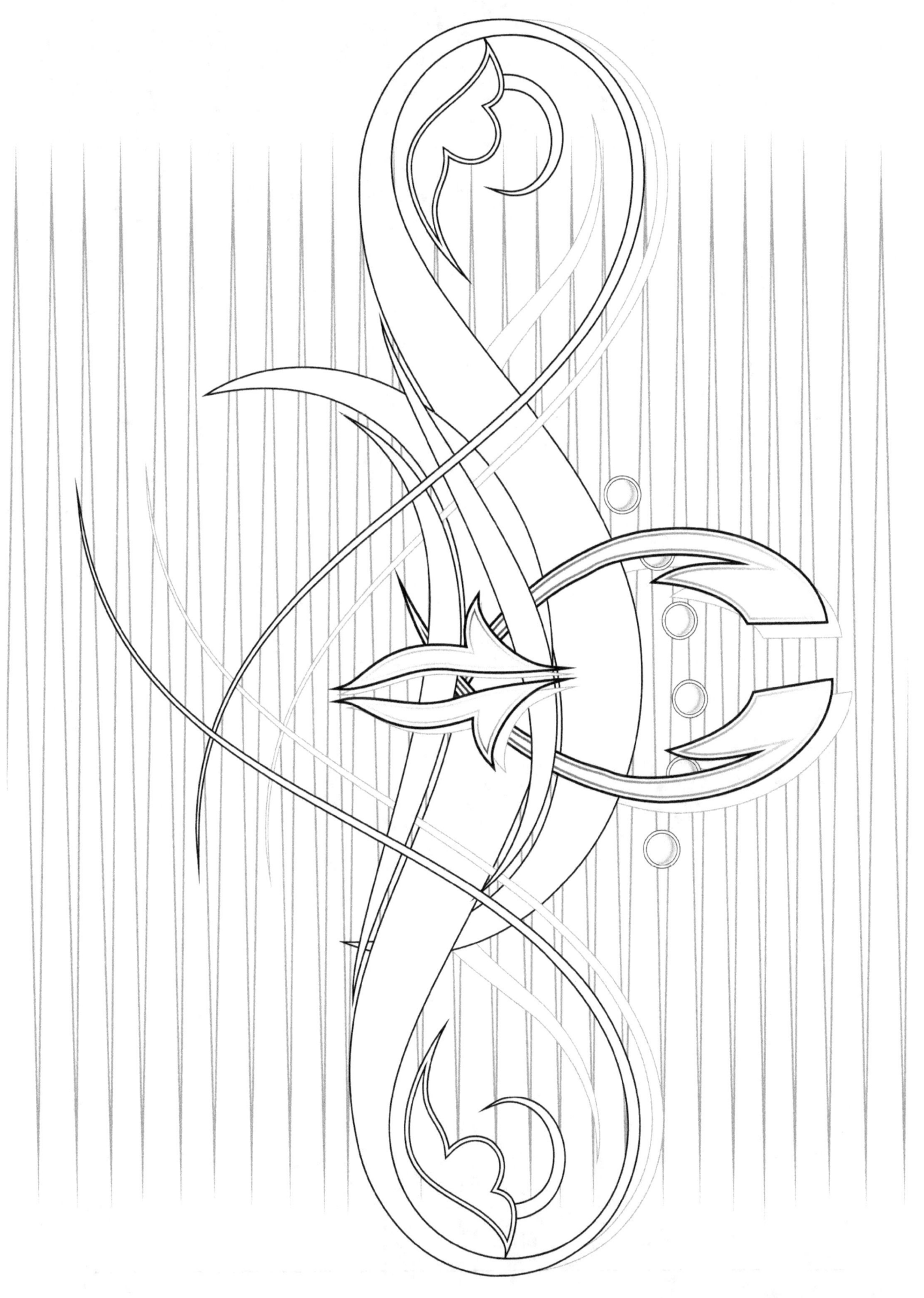

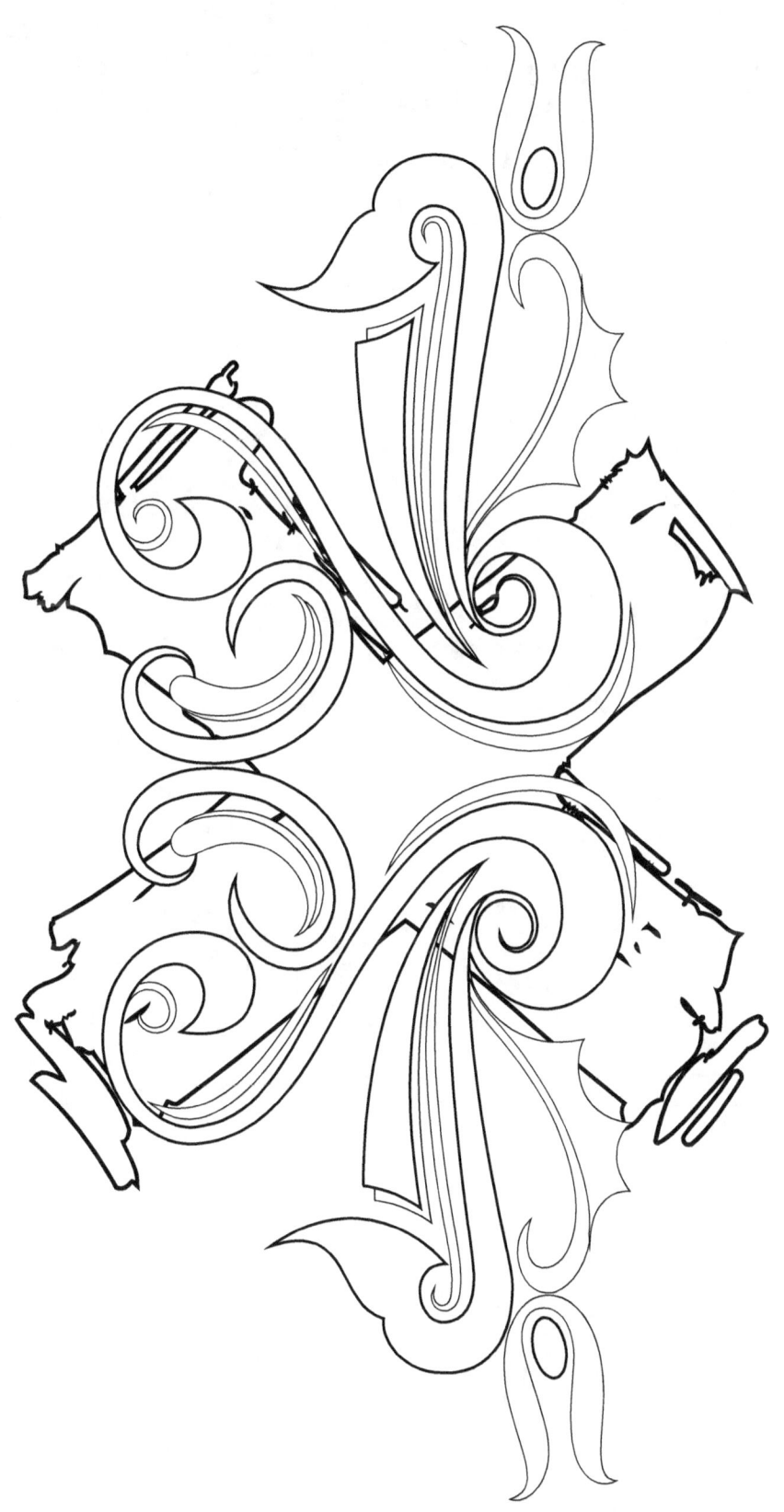

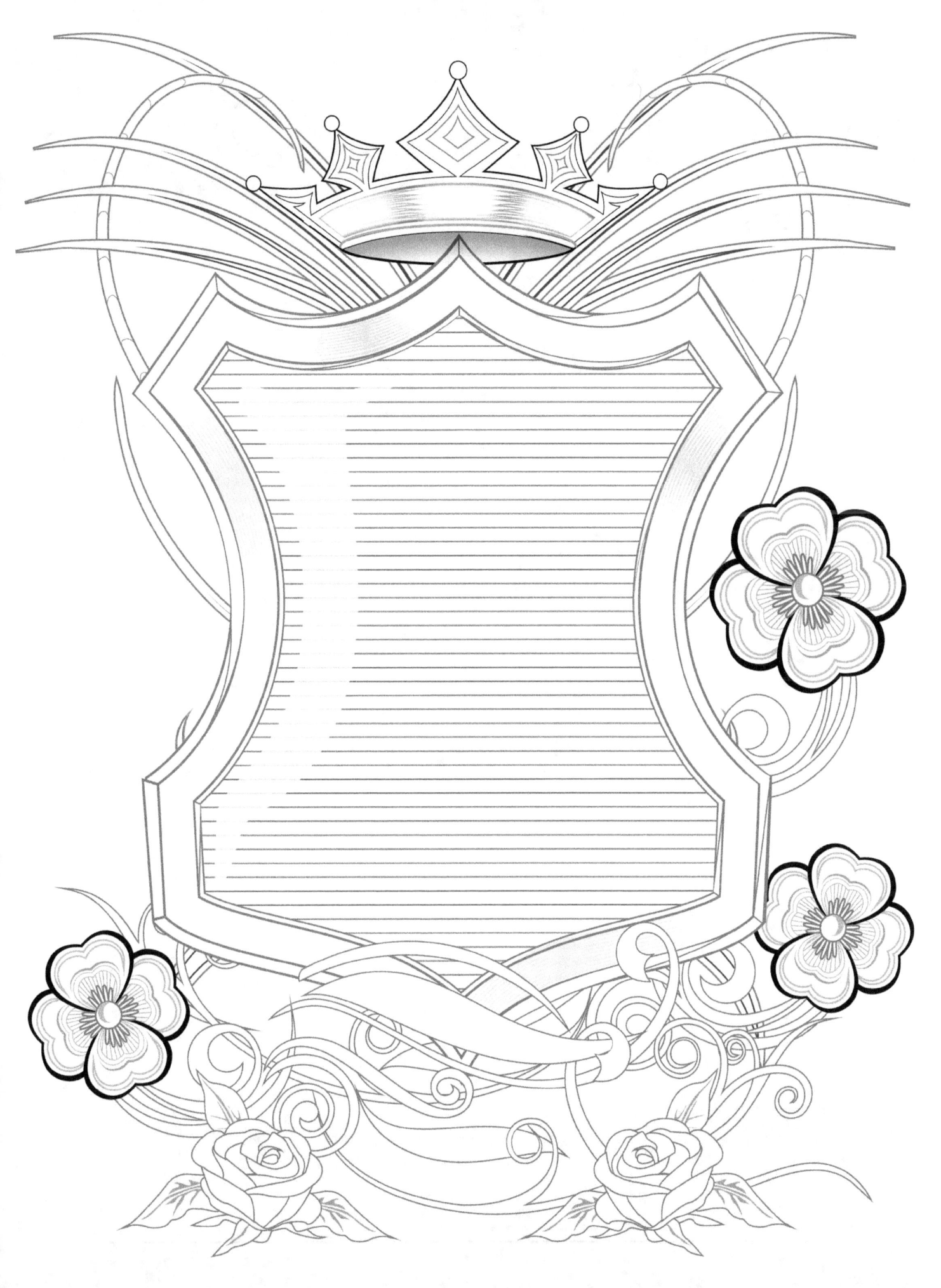

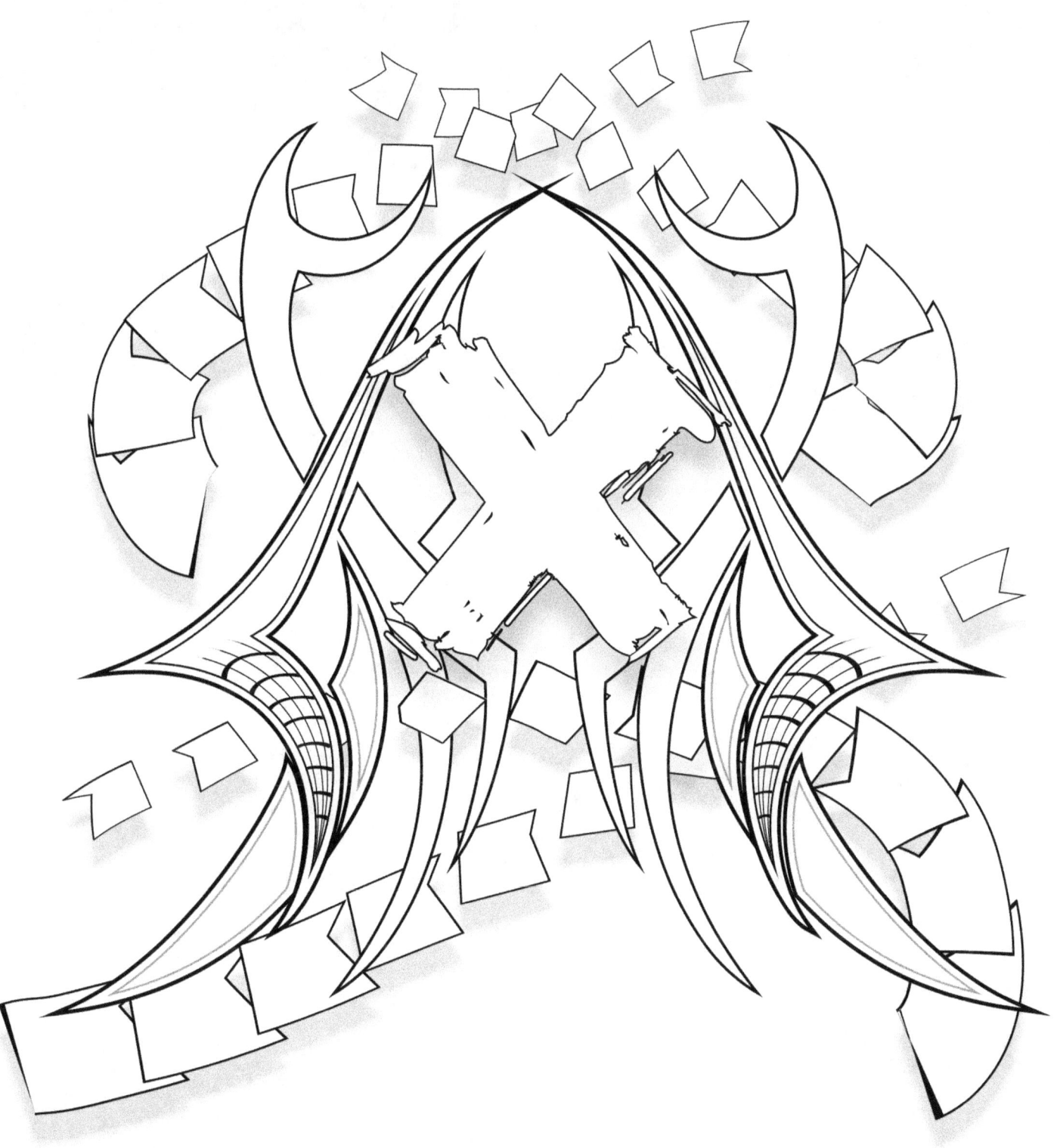

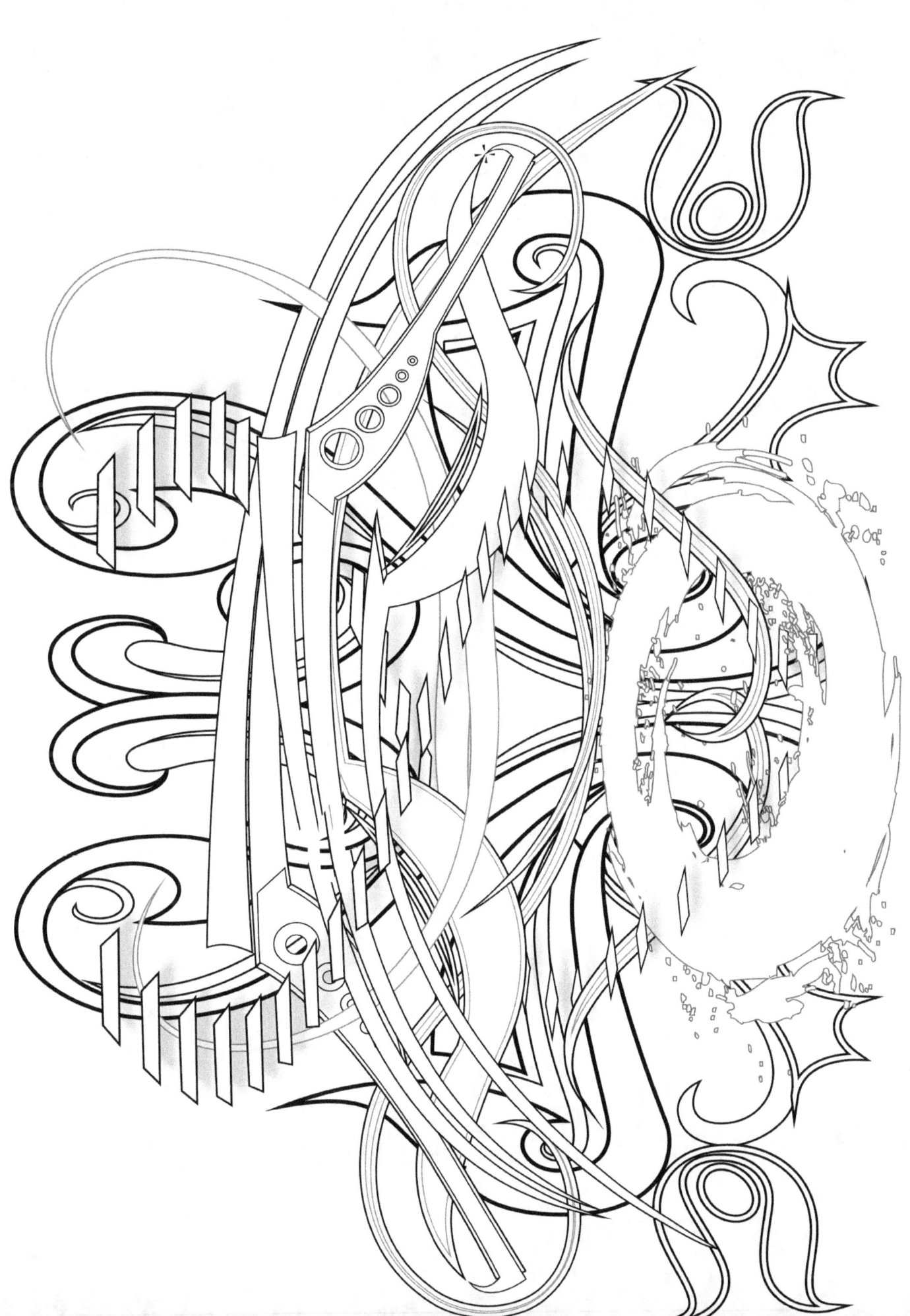

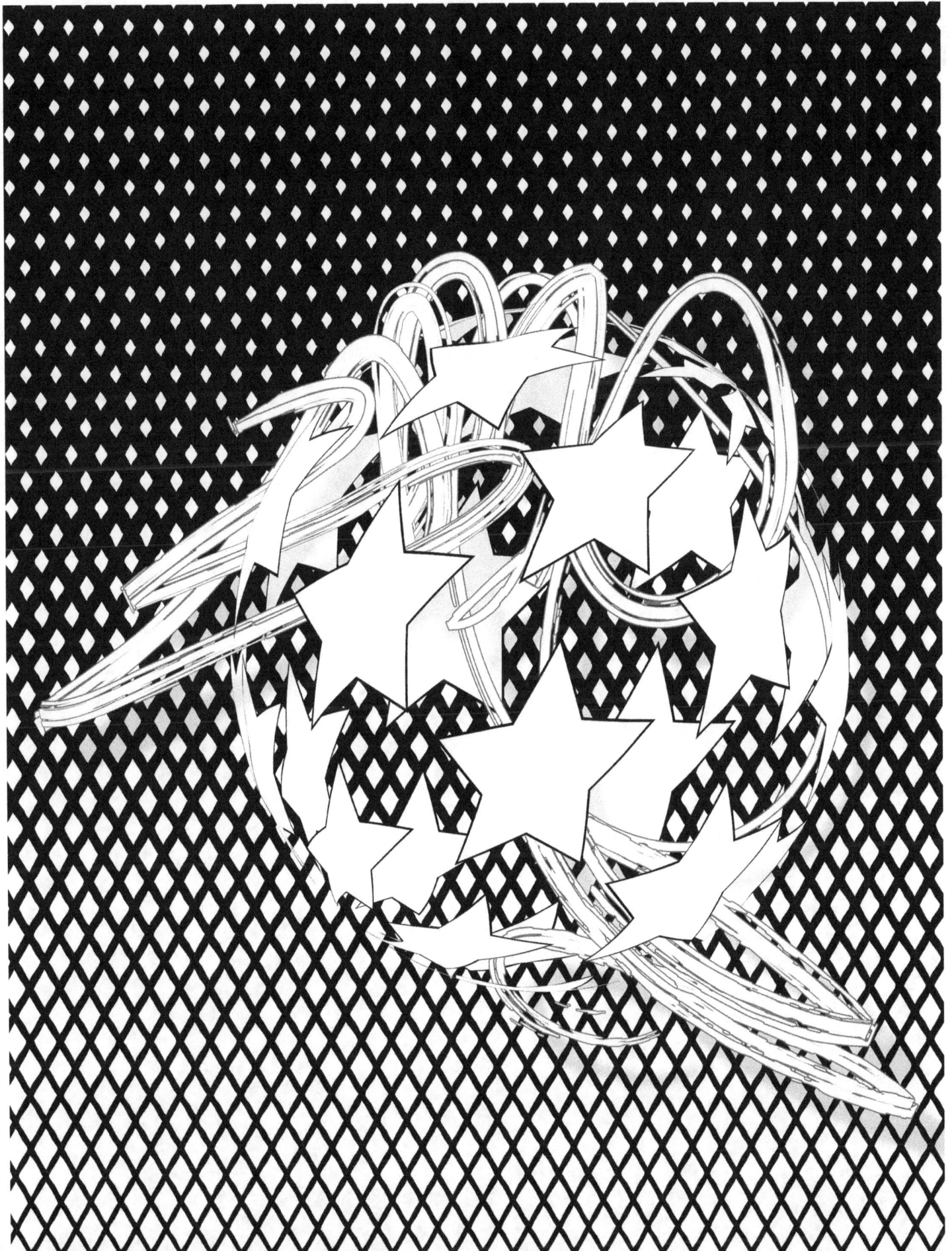

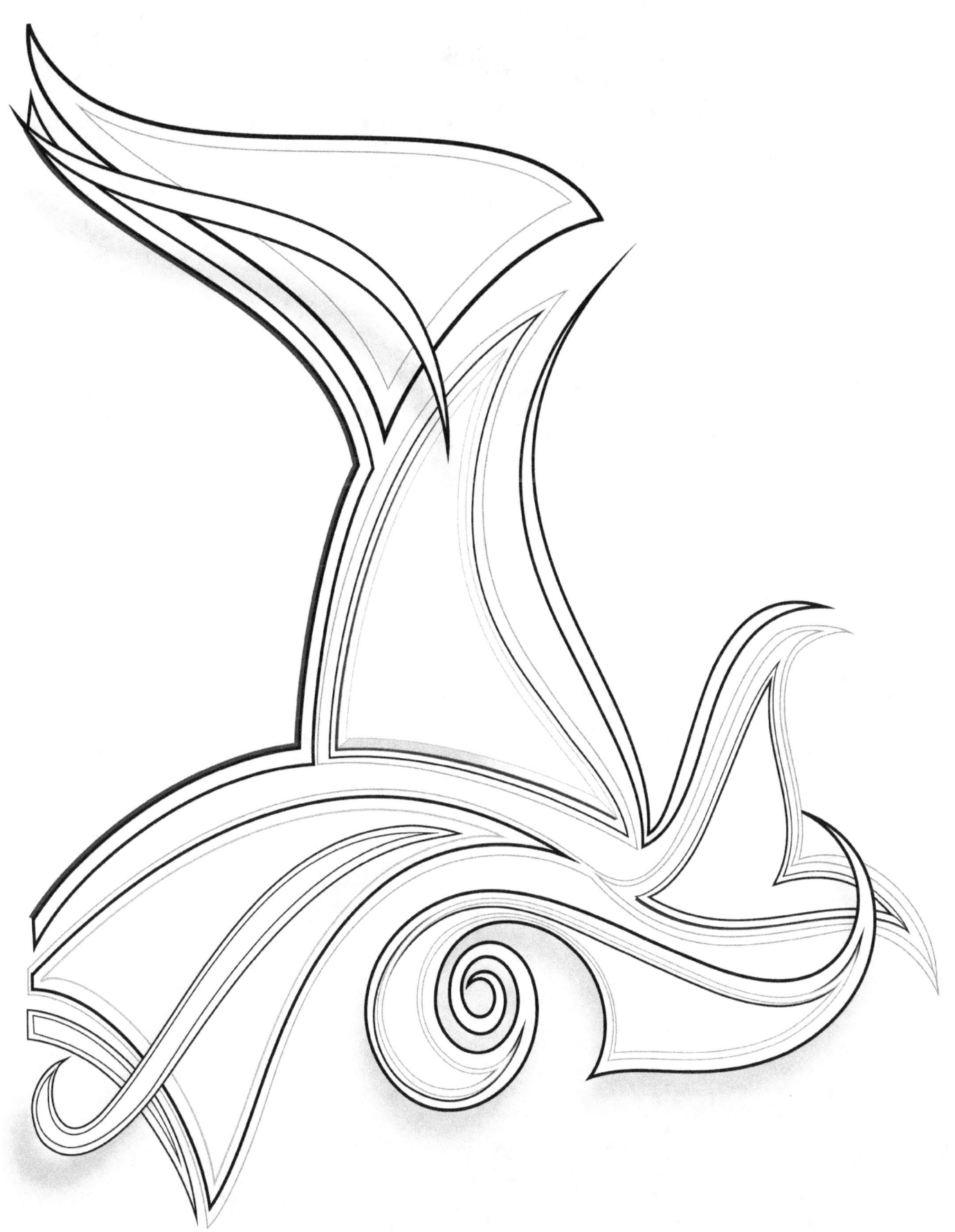

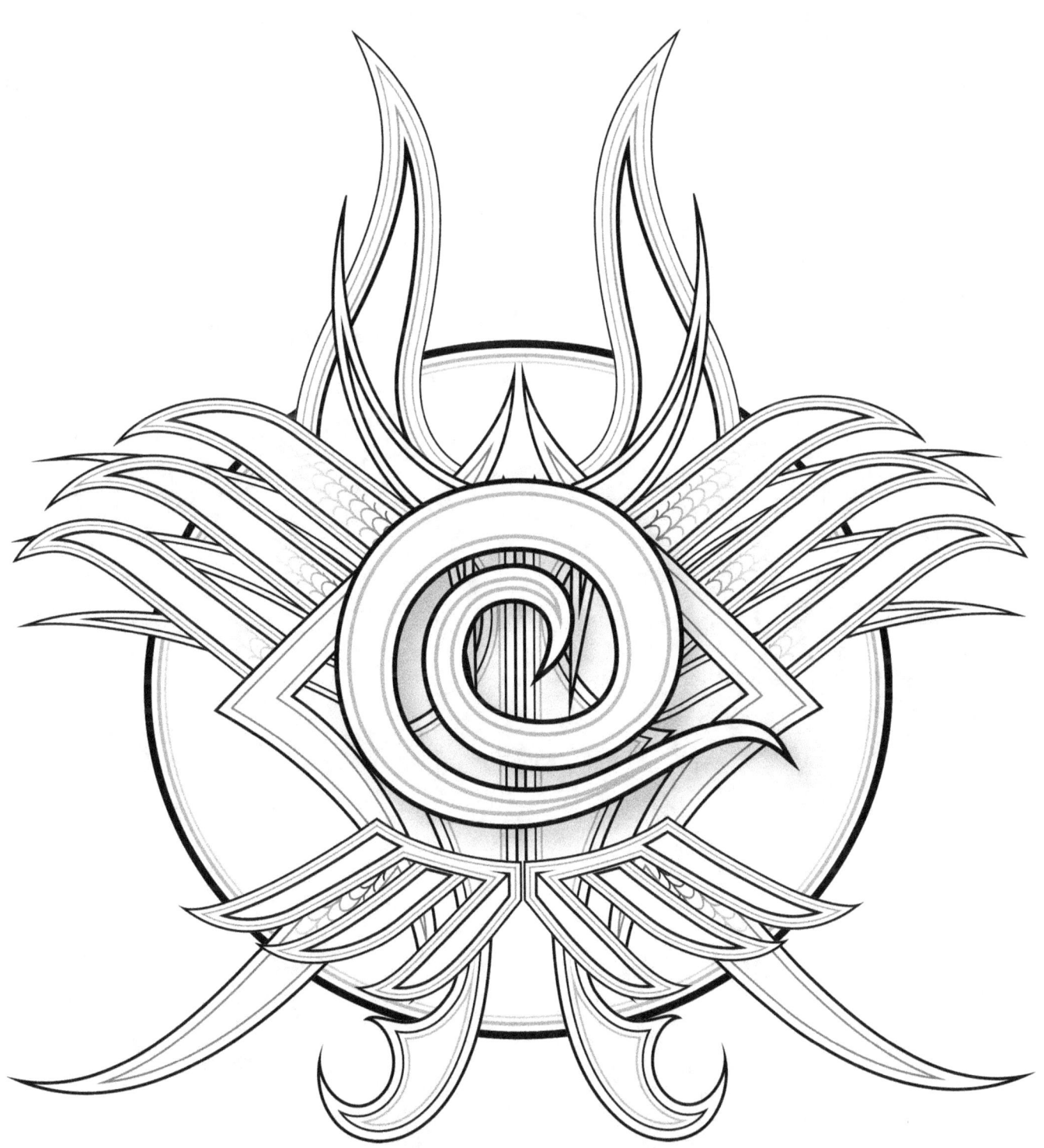

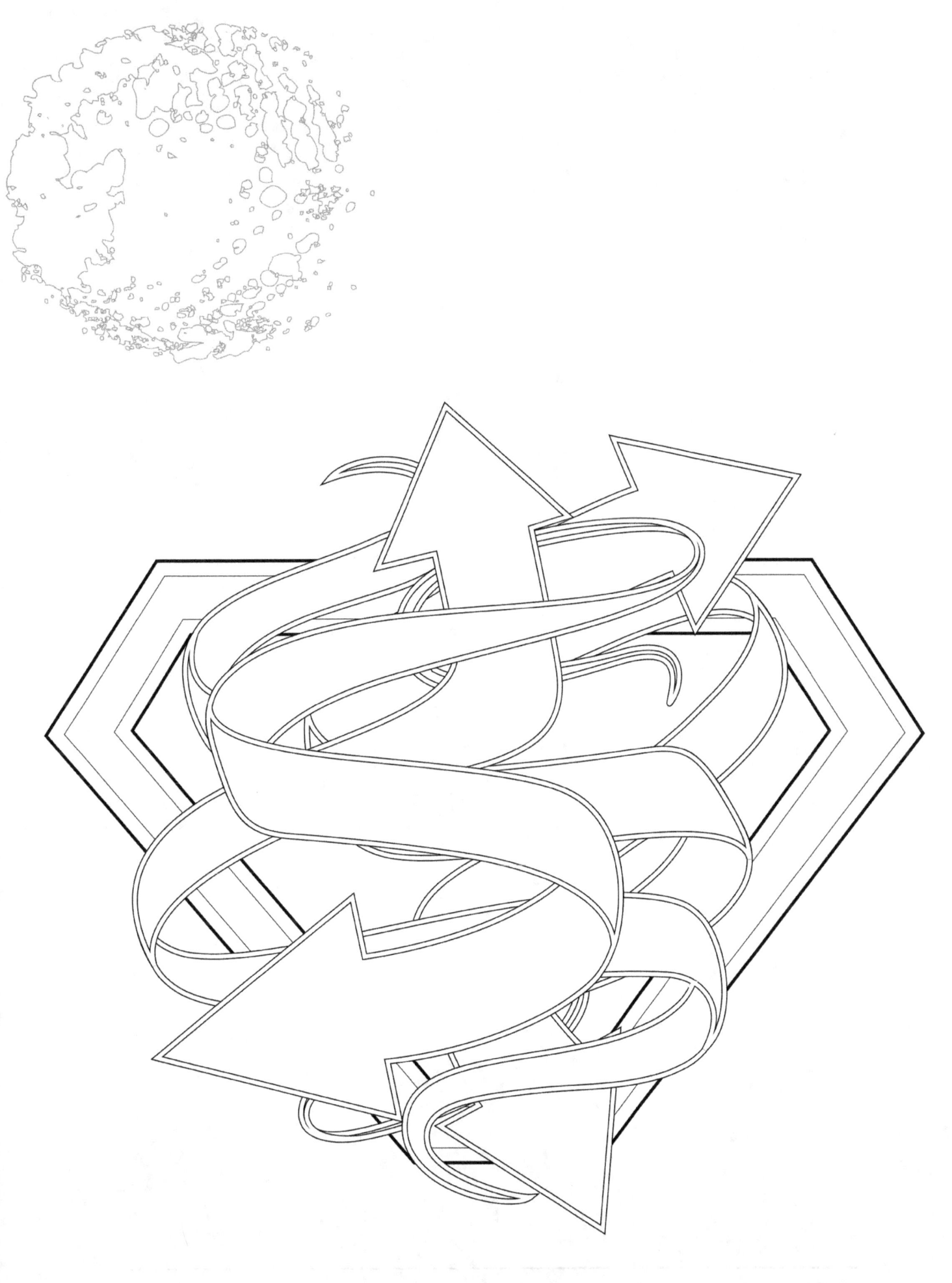

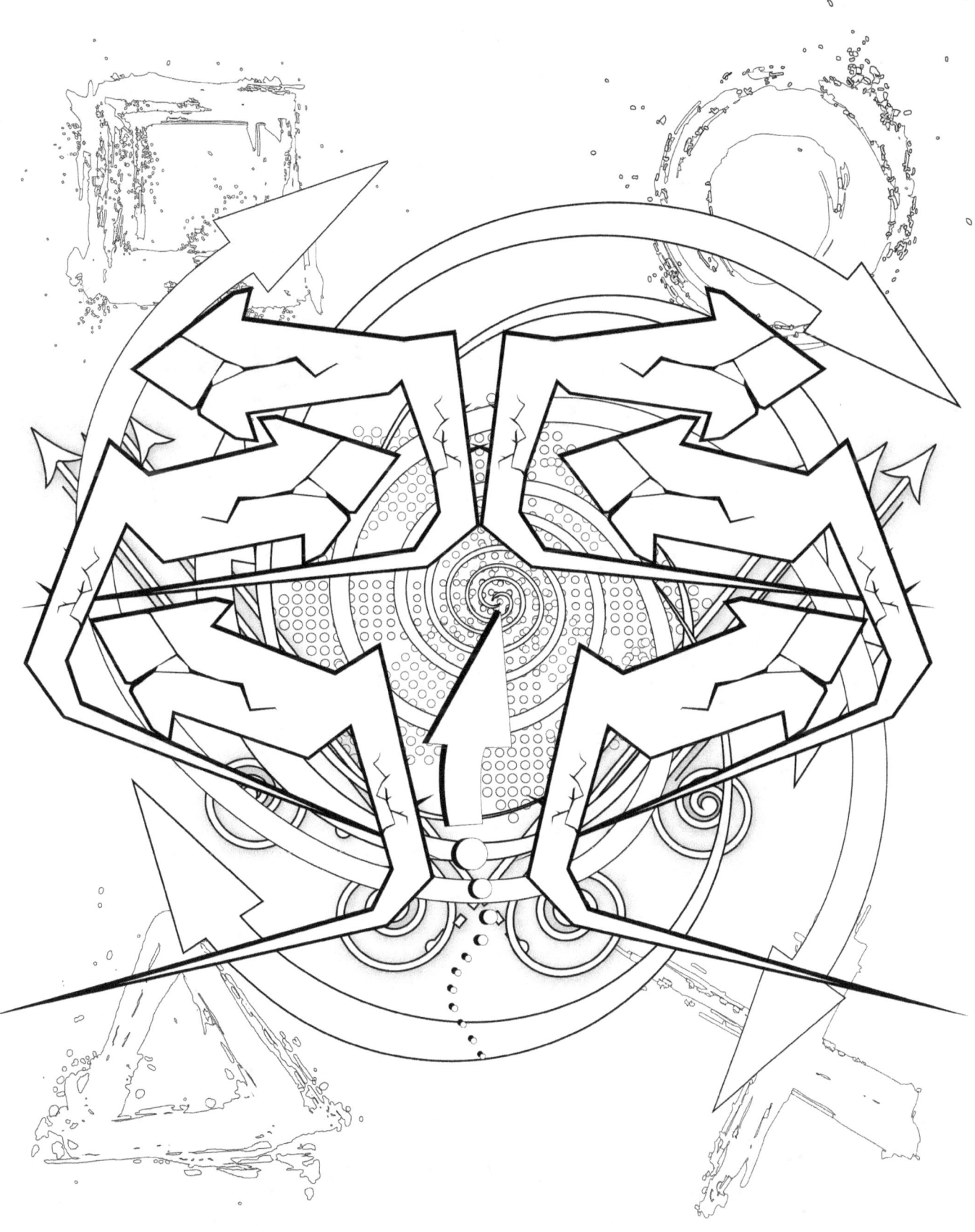

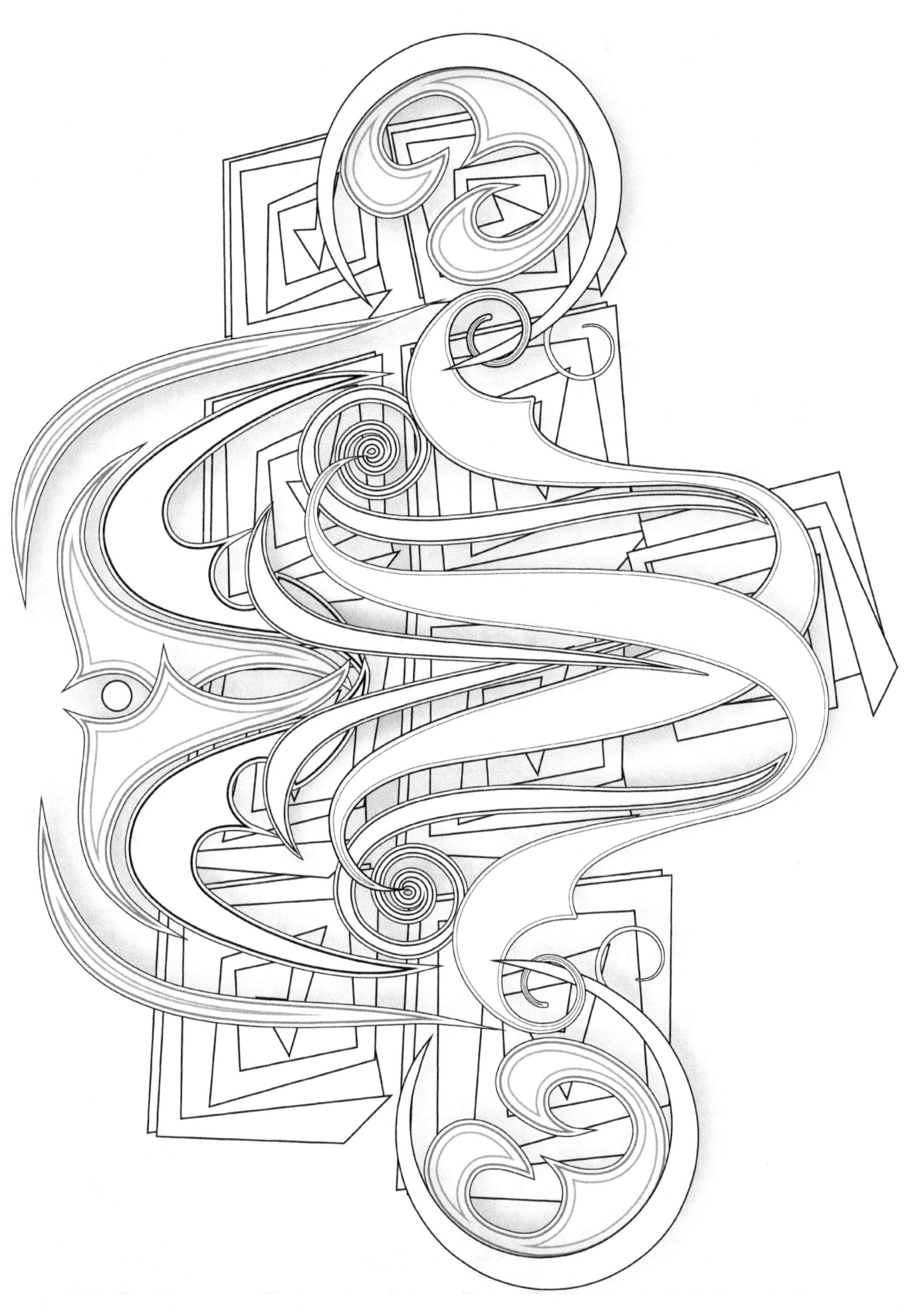

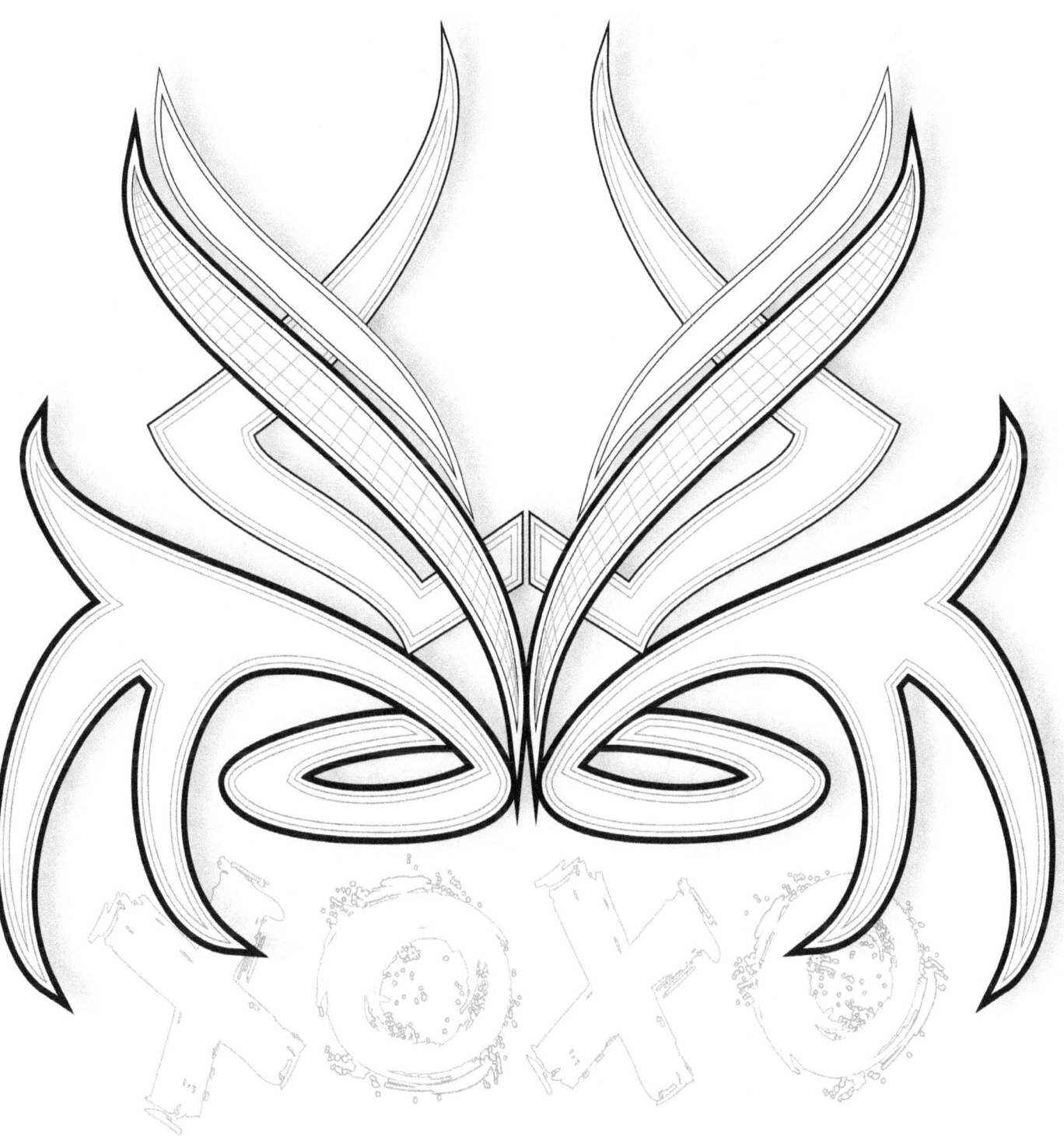

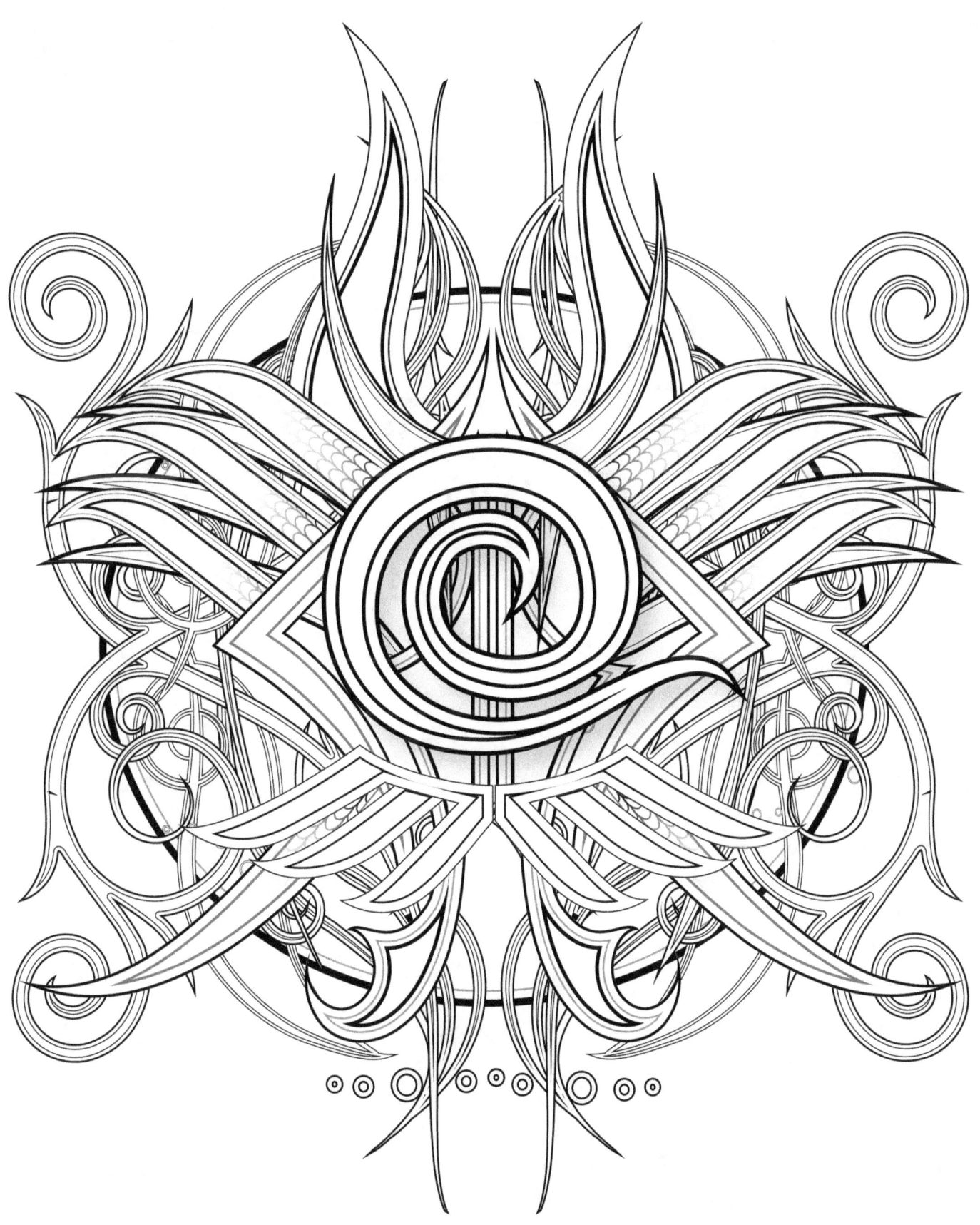

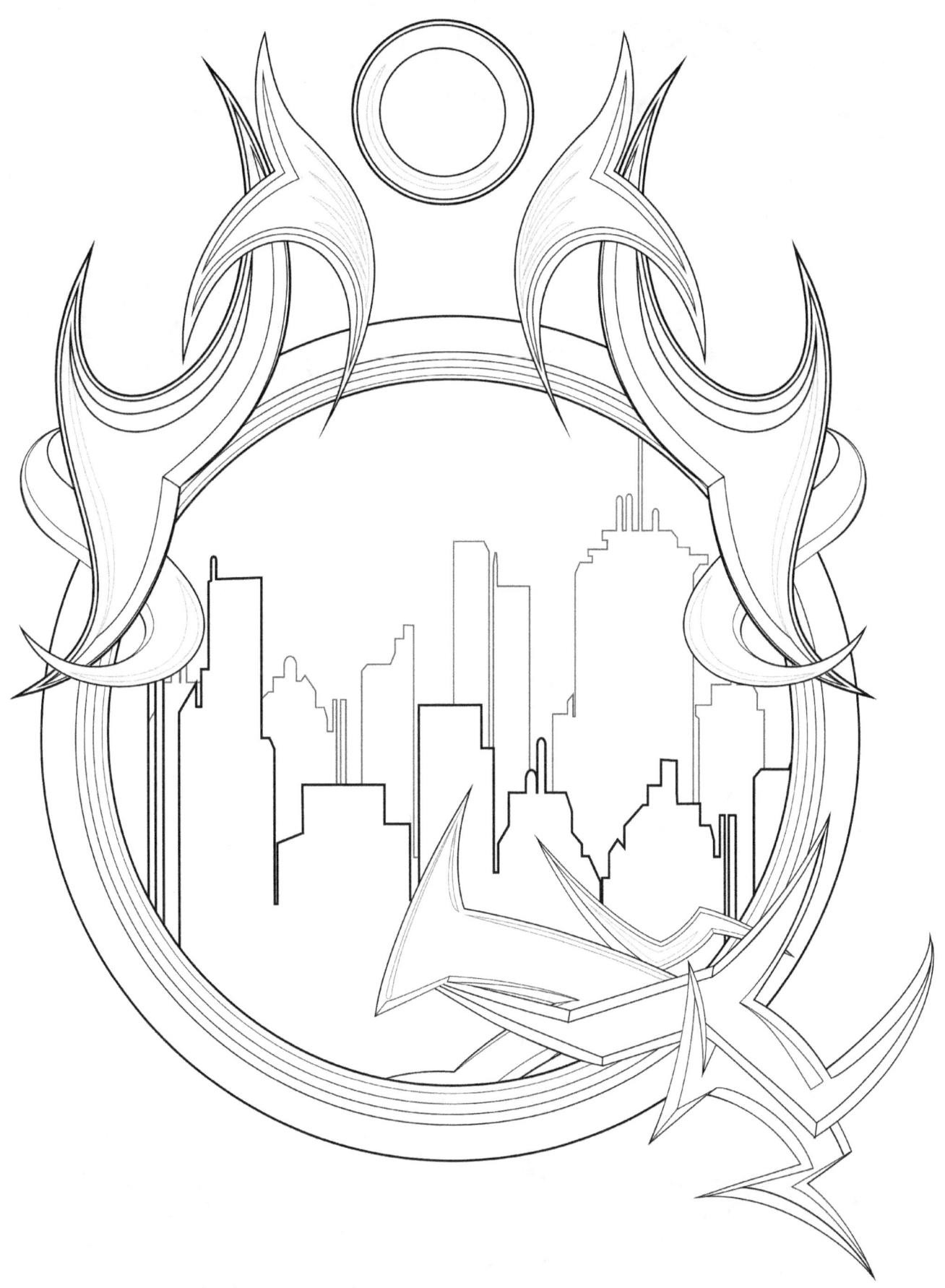

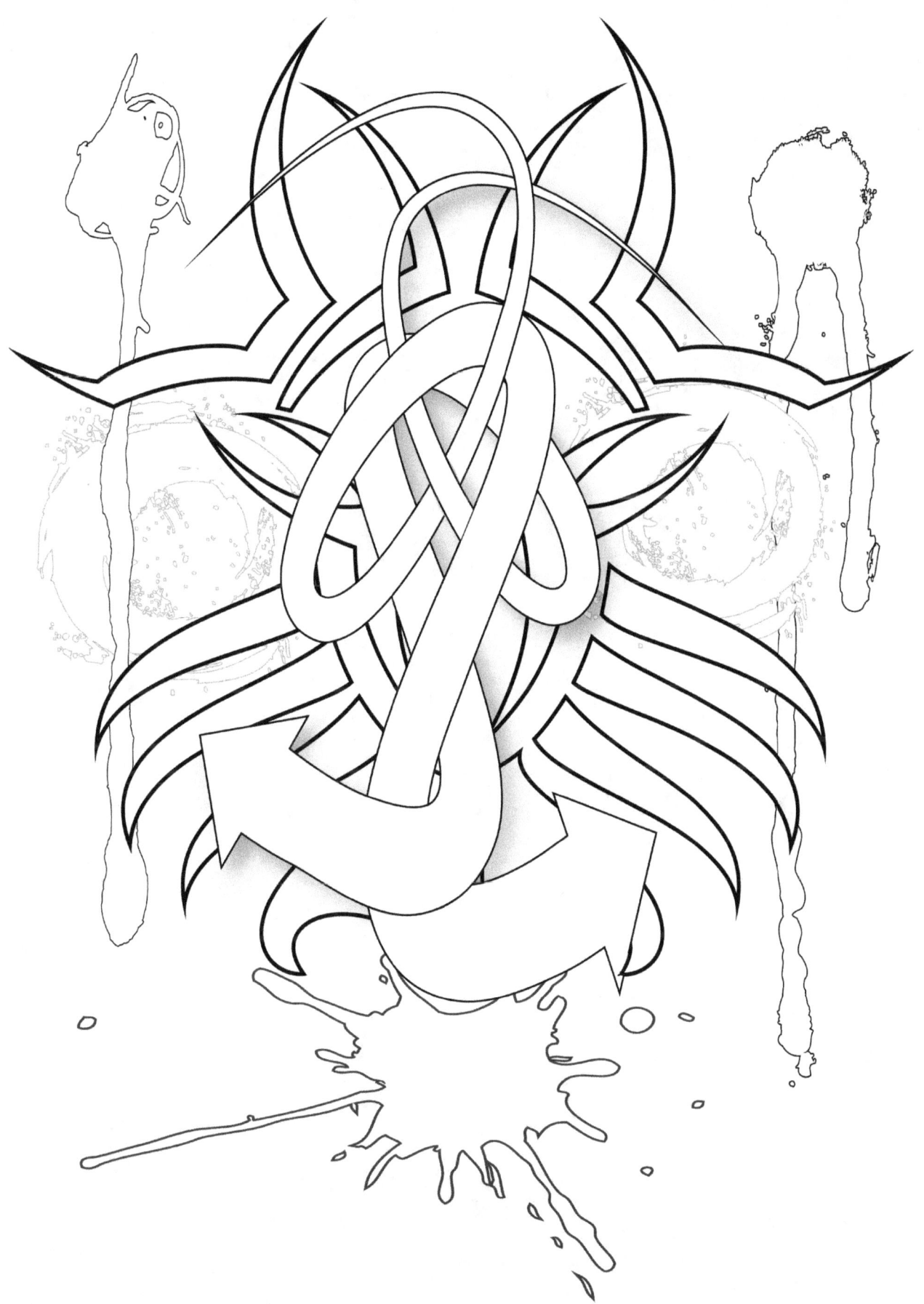

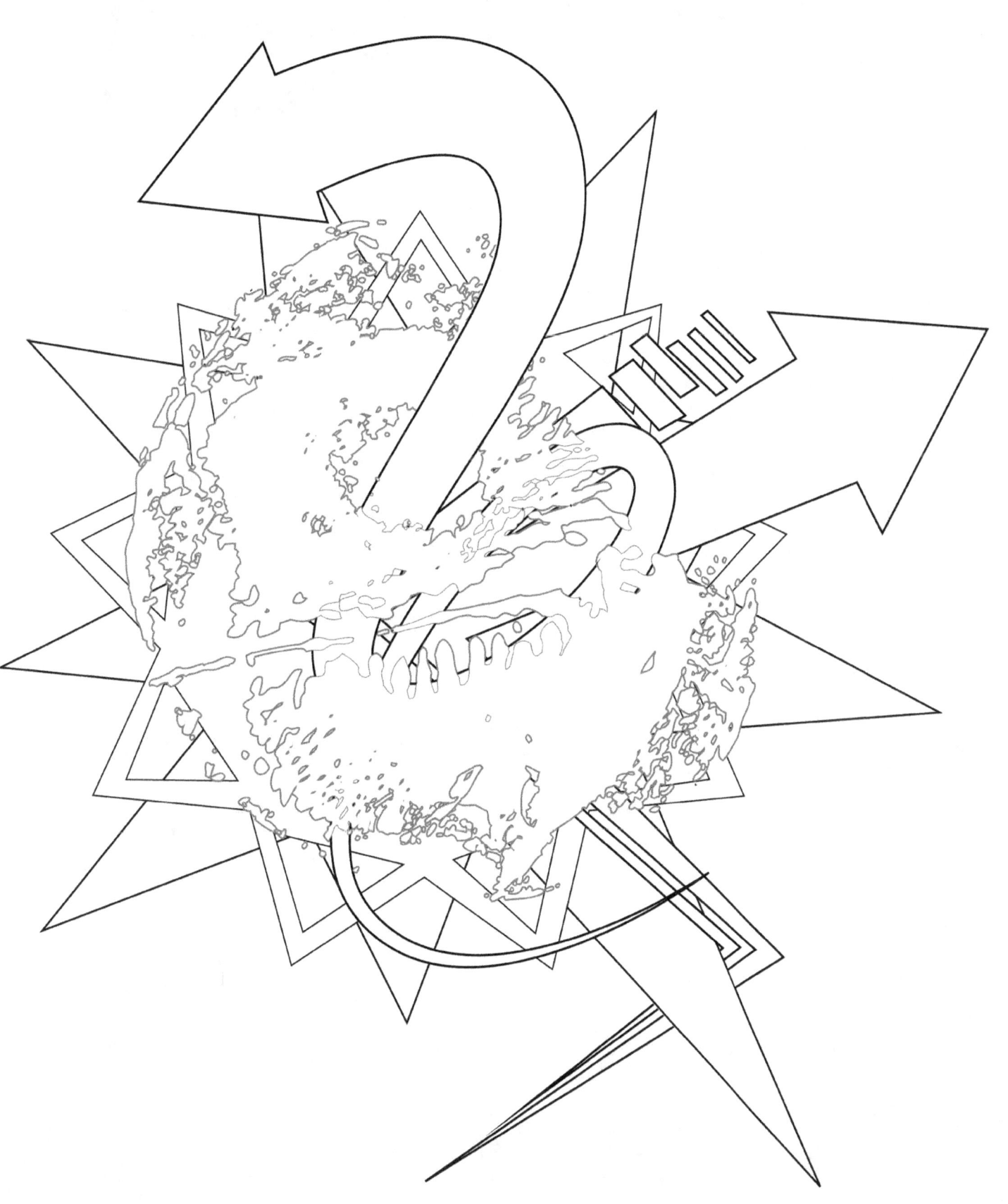

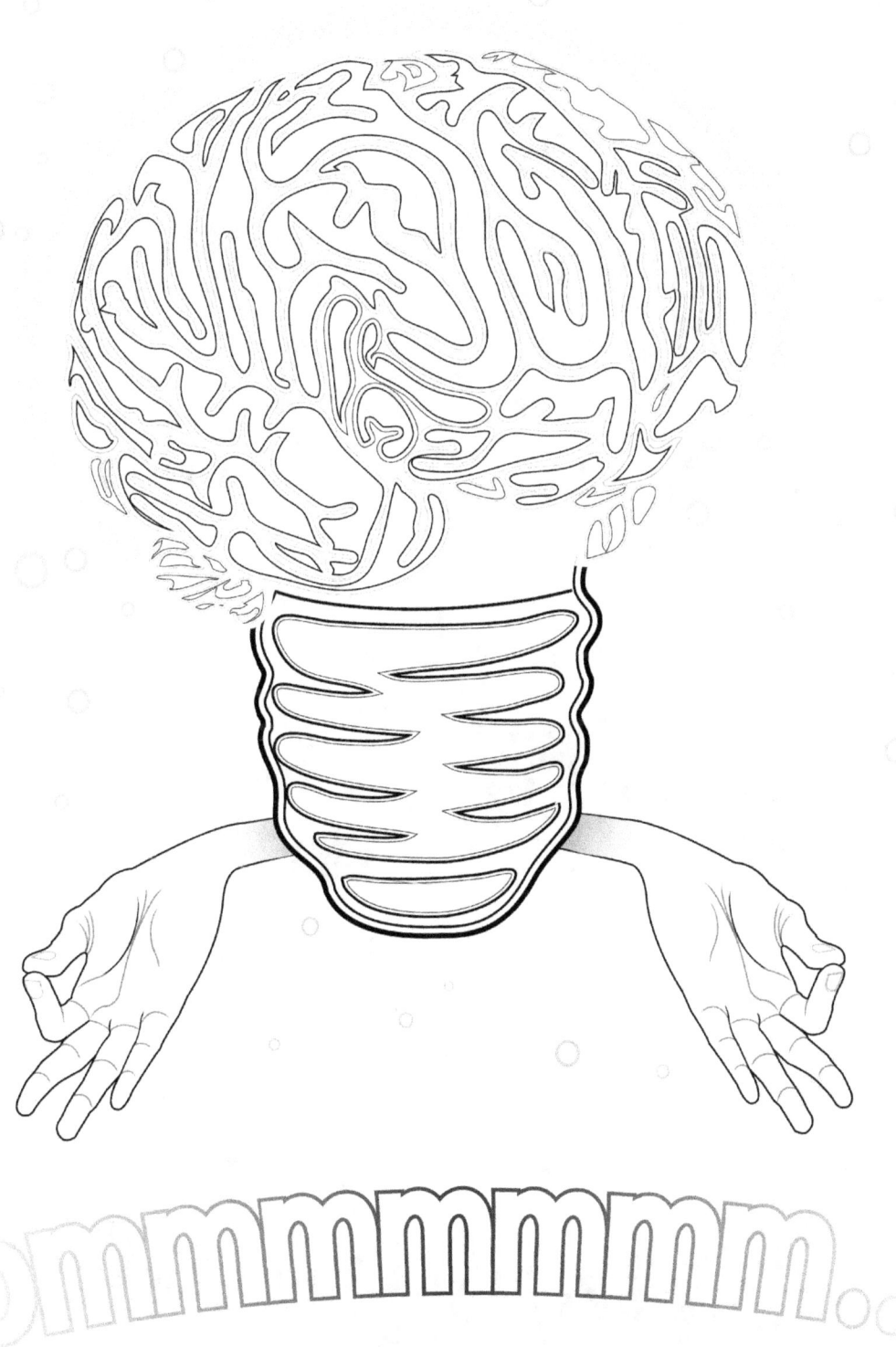

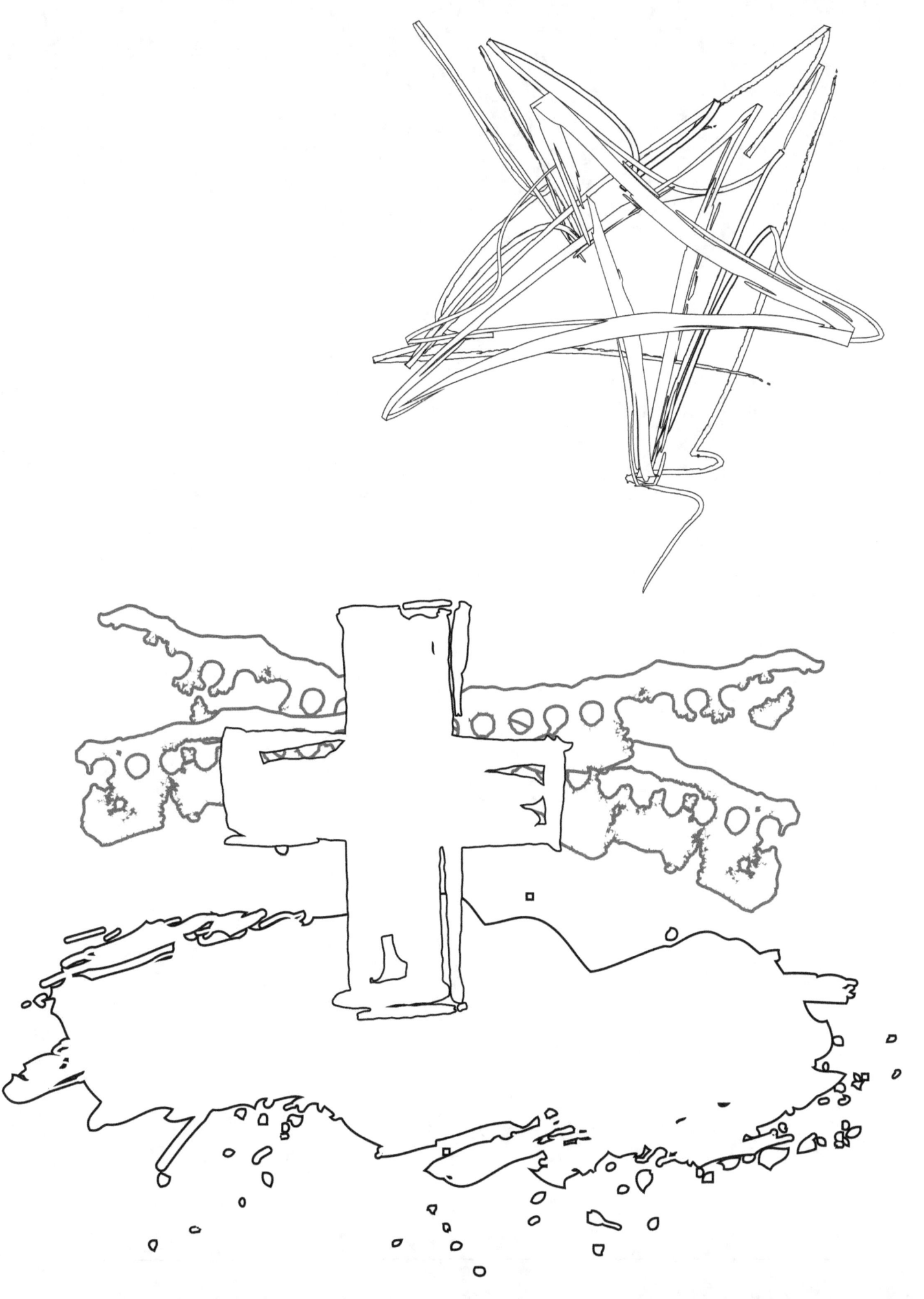

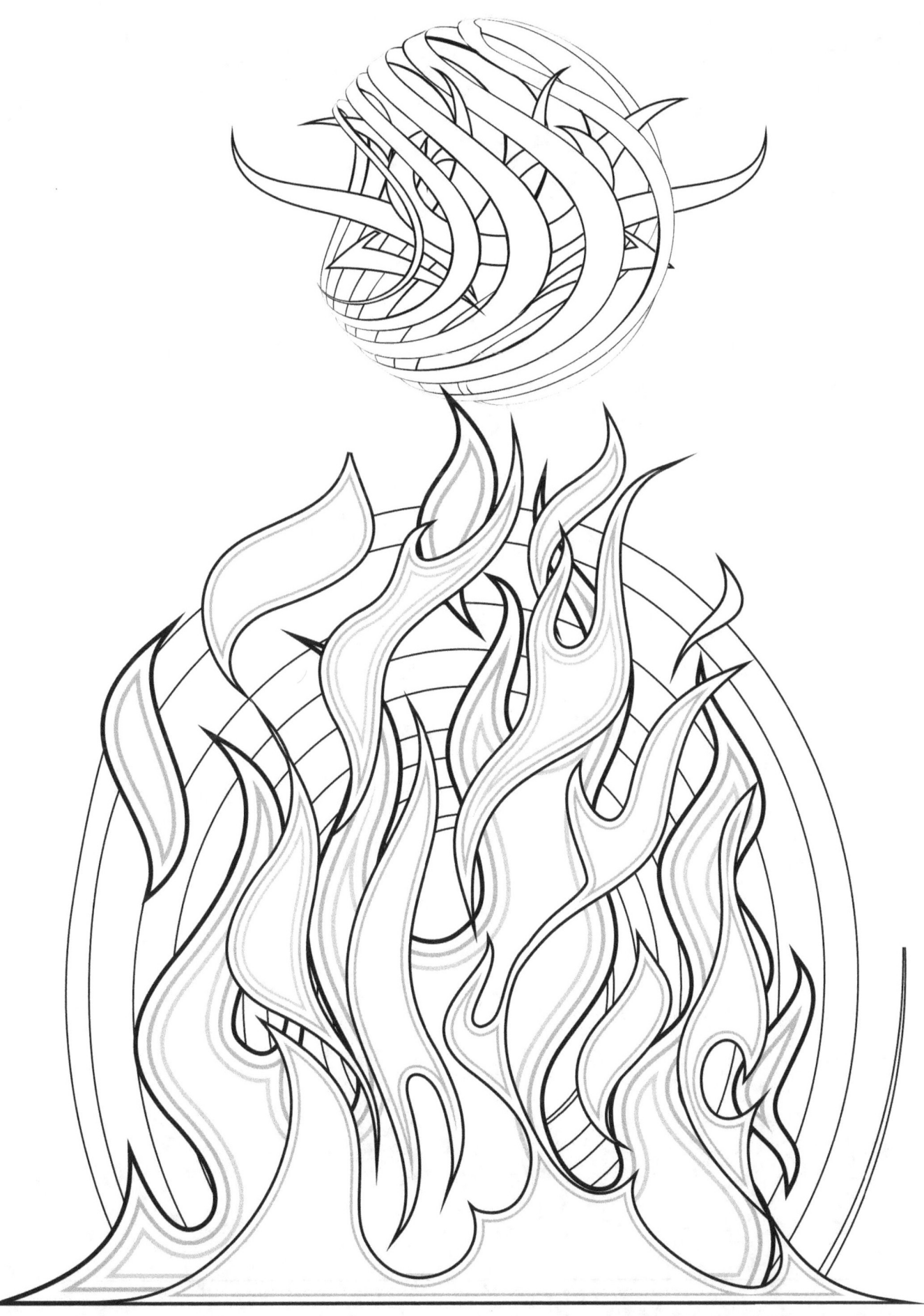

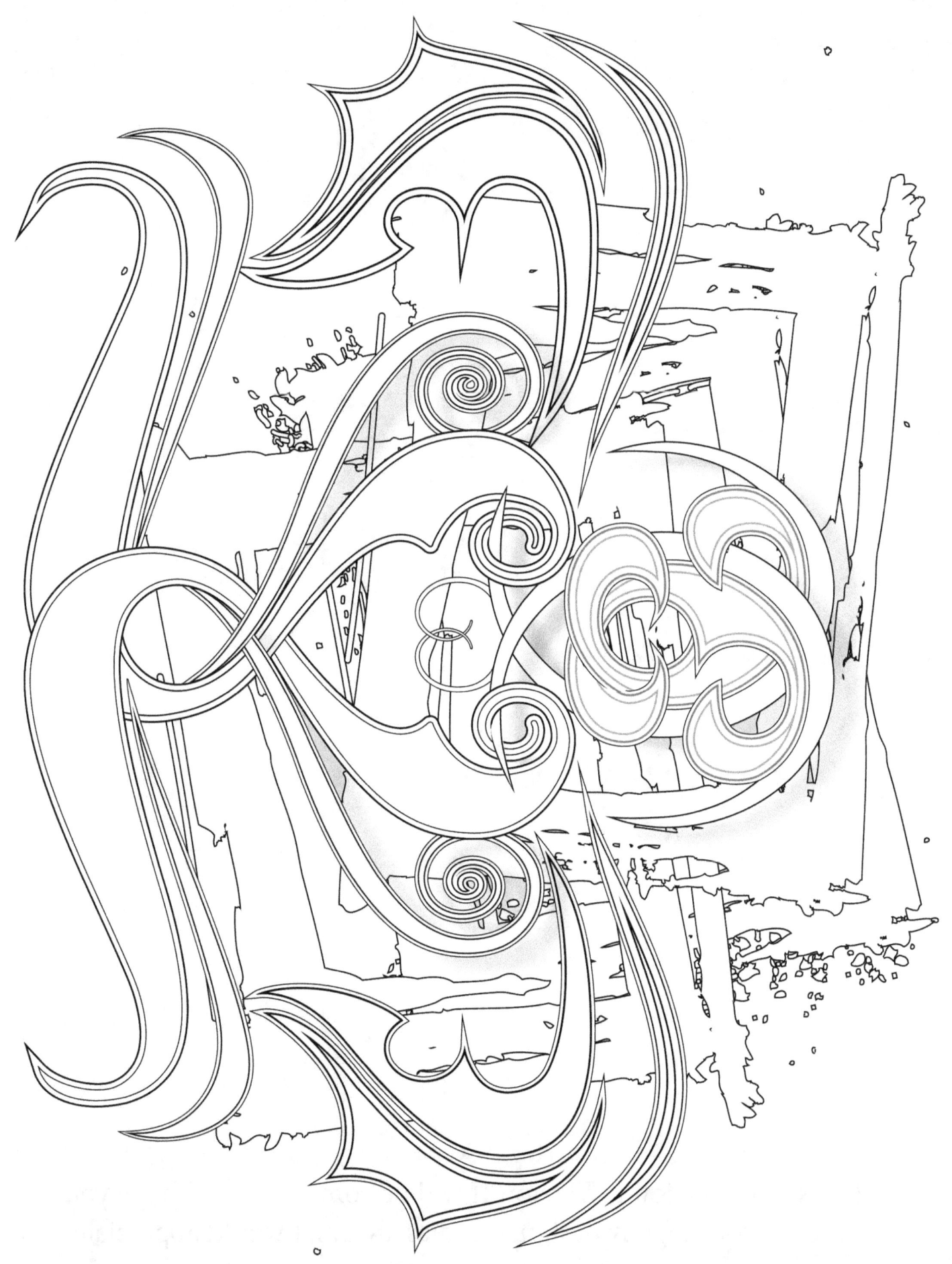

That's it for version I. Version II will be coming soon. I hope you enjoyed coloring my designs. And as always, I would appreciate your review

www.ingramcontent.com/pod-product-compliance
Lightning Source LLC
Chambersburg PA
CBHW080845170526

45158CB00009B/2637